The Ultimate Guide To Starting A Band

How To Start A Band And Be Successful

George K.

Table of Contents

Introduction

Chapter 1 – The Present Situation of the Music Industry

Chapter 2 – How Music Bands Started?

Chapter 3 – Types of Bands

Chapter 4 – Find the Right Band Members

Chapter 5 – Choose the Type of Music for your Band

Chapter 6 – Determine the Band Expenses and Profits

Chapter 7 – Finding the Right Place for Your Band to Practice

Chapter 8 – Musical Instruments You Need for Your Band

Chapter 9 – How to Succeed as a Band

Chapter 10 – Setting Goals and Assigning Tasks

Conclusion

Introduction

I want to thank you for purchasing the book, "The Ultimate Guide to Starting a Band - *How to Start a Band and Be Successful*".

This book provides you guidelines on how to start a band and how to succeed. Chapter 1 describes the music industry, how it started and what companies top the list of successful music makers.

The succeeding chapters will guide you on how to start a band. From finding the band members to the things you need to do to help your band reach the top. Starting a band is not an easy task; it requires a lot of effort, time and dedication in order to succeed.

This book is written to guide you in every phase of starting a band and the problems that you might encounter along the way. If you are serious in putting up a band and you want to succeed, follow the guide provided in this book.

Thanks again for purchasing this book, I hope you enjoy it!

© **Copyright 2014 by George K. - All rights reserved.**

This document is geared towards providing exact and reliable information in regards to the topic and issue covered. The publication is sold with the idea that the publisher is not required to render accounting, officially permitted, or otherwise, qualified services. If advice is necessary, legal or professional, a practiced individual in the profession should be ordered.

- From a Declaration of Principles which was accepted and approved equally by a Committee of the American Bar Association and a Committee of Publishers and Associations.

In no way is it legal to reproduce, duplicate, or transmit any part of this document in either electronic means or in printed format. Recording of this publication is strictly prohibited and any storage of this document is not allowed unless with written permission from the publisher. All rights reserved.

The information provided herein is stated to be truthful and consistent, in that any liability, in terms of inattention or otherwise, by any usage or abuse of any policies, processes, or directions contained within is the solitary and utter responsibility of the recipient reader. Under no circumstances will any legal responsibility or blame be held against the publisher for any reparation, damages, or monetary loss due to the information herein, either directly or indirectly.

Respective authors own all copyrights not held by the publisher.

The information herein is offered for informational purposes solely, and is universal as so. The presentation of the information is without contract or any type of guarantee assurance.

The trademarks that are used are without any consent, and the publication of the trademark is without permission or backing by the trademark owner. All trademarks and brands within this book are for clarifying purposes only and are the owned by the owners themselves, not affiliated with this document.

Chapter 1 – The Present Situation of the Music Industry

The music industry consists of individuals and companies that make money by creating and selling music. Among the many organizations and individuals that are working within the industry are the musicians who create and perform the music, the professionals and companies who compose and sell recorded music, those groups that conduct live music performances, agents who help musicians with their music careers, those who broadcast music, musical instrument manufacturers, educators, and journalists.

The music industry became popular in the middle of the 20th century, when records had replaced sheet music as the biggest trend. In the commercial world, people started talking about the recording industry as a loose synonym of the music industry. Together with their many subsidiaries, the majority of this industry for recording music is controlled by 3 major corporate labels – the Universal Music Group, a French-owned company; Sony Music Entertainment, a Japanese-owned recording company; and Warner Music Group, a US-owned company. Independent labels are those labels outside of these three major labels. The biggest part of the live music market is controlled by the leading promoter and owner of a music venue, the Live Nation. It is the past subsidiary of Clear Channel Communications, the biggest owner of radio stations in the United States. The biggest talent management and booking organization is the Creative Artists Agency.

There has been a drastic change in the music industry since the digital distribution of music was launched. A clear indicator of this is the total music sales − since 2000, the sales of recorded music have dropped significantly, while live music or live bands increased in significance. The biggest music retailer in the world today is digital.

Chapter 2 – How Music Bands Started?

The term band comes from the French word "bande" which means "troop." The main difference between an orchestra and band is that musicians who play in the band play brass, percussion and woodwind instruments. The orchestra includes bowed stringed instruments.

The term band is likewise used to describe a group of individuals who perform together like dance bands. It can likewise be utilized to describe a particular instrument played by a group as in the case of brass bands.

Bands were said to have started in Germany in the 15th century, playing mainly woodwind instruments like oboes and bassoons. At the end of the 18th century, Turkish music or Janissary became popular featuring the instruments like cymbals, large drums, triangles, and flutes. The number of musicians who played in the band also grew during this time. In 1838, a band which consisted of 1,000 wind instrument musicians and 200 drummers performed in Berlin for the Russian emperor.

Band competitions were held. Most were held at Bell Vue, Manchester and Alexandra Palace, London. In 1900, the National Brass Band Festival was held.

During the American Revolutionary War, military bands emerged in the US. The primary role of bands at that time was to go together with soldiers during battles. As the time went by, the role of the military bands lessened, and this marked the advent of town bands. This type of band is made up of local musicians who perform during special events like national holidays. The town bands continued to become popular through the 20th century. At present, several educational institutions in the US have formed marching bands that are composed of students. To promote American bands and music bands, competitions for college and high school bands are held to this day.

Chapter 3 – Types of Bands

As mentioned in Chapter 1, a music band is a group of musicians that get together to perform or sing songs. There are various kinds of bands that use different types of instruments.

Marching Band

This type of band performs at parades, sporting events, and other similar occasions. In the US, there are more high school marching bands than there are college marching bands. They are usually big bands, consisting of about 50-300 members. Normally, the marching bands consist of percussion, trumpets, Mellophones, trombones, sousaphones, and usually flutes, saxophones and clarinets. Percussions are basically made up of snares, bass, drums, cymbals and quads. Most of the marching bands do not include any woodwinds. Marching bands march in straight lines when performing in parades or moving anywhere. They also perform shows where they create images in the field during half-time or in pre-game shows. They lead school songs and cheers in the stands during the games.

Pep Band

This is a type of band that performs in other school sporting or pep events, like pep games, basketball games, and other sports. The majority of universities and high schools have one. These normally include brass, although some may have woodwinds. For percussions, they have snared drums. They are a little bit smaller as compared to marching bands and they are positioned in the stands during indoor games. They lead school cheers and songs.

Concert Band

This is a sit down, indoor band, which normally plays standard repertoire. It is a learning field for young musicians and also for older ones. It comprises a full range of percussions, woodwind, and brass players. It normally consists of thirty to seventy five players, and is a common term for any band that performs indoors.

Symphonic Band

This is a huge indoor ensemble, which consists of sixty to seventy members, which includes full trumpet and clarinet sections. The music is normally thickly scored with not too many solos. The sound they produce is well-blended and complex because it is a big group.

Wind Ensemble

This small indoor ensemble normally comprises only thirty to forty members, with one or two music players on a part. Trumpet and clarinet sections may have only four to six members. It performs a repertoire that is much more scored thinly and has lots of solos.

Jazz Band

This is a common type of band that performs in a jazz style. It usually includes a drum set, trumpets, piano, bass, and saxophones. They perform only jazz music, which is done in swing style. Piano and bass figure prominently in the style, and there are lots of solos. There are various types of jazz bands, including big band and cool jazz.

Chapter 4 –Find the Right Band Members

In forming a band, the first step you need to do is find the right band members to help you bring the band to life. Finding the right members is very important to your success. But where do you start your search? Here are tips that can help you find the right individuals for your band.

Ask Your Friends Around

Your bandmates could be just around the corner – you just don't know they are there. Some of your friends might be in the band already and are looking for a change, or they might know someone who is looking for a gig. The good thing about finding a bandmate is that you know the deal about the person before they join the band. Your friends might know a great bass player that was never given a chance to show his skills; this is a good chance for him to show you his talent. Searching for band members via your local music scene group means you are more confident that you will find someone dependable – or at least have a good lead.

The Record Shop

Where do most music lovers gather? Of course in the record store, in the instrument shop or other music related shops. The majority of these areas, particularly the ones owned independently, have message boards where you can put your ads for recruiting band members. Make sure that you put something about the music that you want on the ads, or at least some information concerning the band that you want to put up and don't forget to include how interested people can contact you. You can also ask the staff of these stores if they know someone who is looking for a band.

The Internet

There are websites that are filled with ads from individuals searching for a band to join. Check the lists of musicians in your area who are interested in searching for a band with whom to play, and put your own advertisement looking for band members. Put the same information you would on an ad on the record store message board. You can check out the musician's forums.

Rehearsal or Studio Rooms

Call a rehearsal or recording studio in your area and let the people know that you are searching for musicians. Check out if they have an area where you can visit and post ads for your band. The personnel working at these places are aware who is playing with which band and who are in search for a new gig, and they could be a good source. Even if you haven't used the rehearsal or studio space before, don't hesitate to approach them in your search of finding the right band members.

Distribute Your Ads

Stick ads or posters all over town, in areas where you think most musicians normally visit. Book shops, clubs, venues, and coffee shops – the secret is to let people know that you are looking for band members.

How to Narrow Down Your List of Potential Band Members?

You have a list of musicians who want to be a member of your band. The most difficult part is deciding which will be the right people for your band. Here are tips on how you can narrow down your choices.

Level of Commitment

Determine the potential band member's level of commitment. You prefer someone who is in the same commitment level as the rest of the members do. Is the band just jamming for fun during the weekends or is a full-time thing for the potential band members? Musicians who have high level of commitment are always good, but they can get discouraged if the other members are lazy and want to play only at minimal times. Determine how often the band will be playing and then look for the one that can commit to that schedule.

Technical Capabilities versus Diversity

Although technical capabilities are essential, there should be also a good balance between music diversification. Anyone can get a guitar and shred just like Yngwie Malmsteen with the right amount of practice using the same notes again and again, but not all can play such an instrument like Jimi Hendrix could.

Love Playing the Same Style of Music

The right band members should enjoy playing the same style of music as the rest of the band members do.

Compatibility with Personality

Being a band member is about having fun and you should be able to get along well with all the members of the band. Generally speaking, you should be able to get along with individuals within your age group better, thus you can consider this when choosing the band members.

Open-Minded to Different Kind of Music

Although this may be not applicable to every band, it is a good idea to consider this when finding a band member, if your band decides to modify its musical path.

Band Playing Experience

Basically, the more band playing experiences the better. There is a great variation between self-taught band members that practice on their own at home and those who learned with the help of other musicians. Those musicians without the experience at all will have a hard time following songs since they are used to playing at home with DVD's. Also, if your band plans to perform live gigs, musicians with minimal experience will have stage freight.

Interest

Does the potential band member take the band seriously that they will prioritize it? Can the potential band members should be able to contribute a lot to the band musically? Interest is shown if they can help a lot in turning the ideas into the songs and take additional practice at home as well. If the musician is always late for practices, only plays what they are told to play and does not contribute, then the possibilities is that the musician is not at all committed to the band.

Chapter 5 - Choose the Type of Music for your Band

Choose your genre. If in case the band members cannot agree on one genre, you can pick two or three genres or you can mix it together and create your own genre. Choose a genre that you and your band members can play well and that your soloist sounds good when singing. Your band can start with simple songs and different kinds of genre in the beginning and see what fits the group abilities and likes.

Classical Music

This type of music was considered as the music of the old days. Classical music is normally played in a giant auditorium, with a conductor frantically waving his staff and most of the time wears black clothes. It is further categorized as follows:

>**Orchestral Music** – a grand collection of many musicians, grouped based on the instrument they are handling, years of training and practice, guided by their sheet music and the conductor. This group started in the 17th century.

Chamber Music – it comprises of smaller instrumental arrangement.

Opera – this type of classical music was introduced during the Baroque era. The group normally accompanies an act, or shows the emotions of a character on a well-constructed background.

Rock Music

The popular celebrity associated with this genre is Elvis Presley, followed by Little Richard and Chuck Berry. This genre is further categorized into the following styles or types. Keep in mind that they are more of less styles of rock instead of completely different genres, and that a band or artist can be found in more than single style.

Alternative rock – is seen only for a short period of time and was out of the ordinary, even by rock standards. This can be defined more of movements instead of individual bands.

Art Rock – the early form of progressive rock and psychedelic rock.

Arena Rock – it is a different way to display the talent of rock bands, under dynamic stage acts, crowd inclusion and heavy lighting. The style concentrates more on the stage as compared to any band in particular.

Metal Rock – is the branch of rock with the most number of offshoots. It is initiated by Black Sabbath.

Glam Rock – includes a wider range of other types of rock, and adds promiscuity and feminine detailing. An example of this includes the music of Elton John, T. Rex and David Bowie.

Blues

Blues is a musical genre and form that started in African-American communities in the United States in the Deep South at the end of the 19th century from field hollers, shouts and chants, spirituals, rhymed simple narrative ballads, spirituals, and work songs. This style is everywhere, even rock and roll, jazz, and rhythm and blues, is characterized by particular chord progressions of which the twelve bar blues is the most popular. The blue notes are played or sung flattened or slowly bent in relation to the pitch of the primary scale, are likewise an essential part of the sound.

Jazz

The second genre born from African conventional music. It is believed to be America's first indigenous type of music. It started out after the Civil War; the black individuals were free to seek employment and travel.

Electronic

This type of music is much older than you think. Thaddeus Cahill was the first in the electronic music and his telharmonium in 1897. It started using the idea of electronically produced music to generate scores that were hard to replicate by man using the present mechanical instrument.

Folk

This type of music is classified into two groups, folk revival and traditional folk. It is something that is indigenous to a culture, popularized at events and is passed down most of the time orally. The songs are anonymously sourced and are therefore, not owned by anyone.

Country

This type of song originated in 1920. It is a combination of blues music, gospel and southern folk songs. This genre was made popular by Jimmie Rodgers, who is likewise known as the Father of Country music.

Rhythm and Blues

This is often abbreviated as R&B, a genre that originated in the 1940s in African-American communities. Record companies used the term to describe recordings marketed to urban African-Americans during the time when jazz, urbane, rocking based music with an insistent heavy beat was starting to become popular. The term has undergone several shifts in meaning. For instance, in the early 1950s, it was applied frequently to blues records.

Chapter 6 – Determine the Band Expenses and Profits

Another important thing that you need to discuss with your band members is not a fun matter to talk about – money. The band member's relationship can be easily affected by monetary matters, so even if you are not very serious about your band, it is important to discuss about finances. Here are some of the things that you need to discuss with the band members that involve money matters.

- If you are forming the band not to make money, that's fine. However, once the prospect arises (the talent show prize, a paid gig), you should talk about it before it happens.

- Discuss on how you will split up the profit. Who will get a higher percentage? Be advised that you should proceed with caution when discussing this as it is a rather touchy subject.

- Income from various sources can be divided in different ways. The performance earnings can be divided evenly, but the songwriter will get more depending on the sales.

- If you hire a manager, he normally gets 10 to 15%. Even if the manager is your friend, this should apply. Since you are just starting out, there is no need for you to hire a manager yet.

- The band should think of the expenses – rehearsal space, recording studio, music instruments, and others. You need to save a part of your earnings so you will have funds for these expenses.

- Decide who will spend the money. If you need to pay for the rehearsal space, where will you get the money? How will you divide these expenses?

- If needed, contracts and lawyers can make terms official and keep everyone involved protected. Don't be afraid to mention the possibility of a contract - it is quite common in the music industry.

When it comes to money matters, the more you know about it, the less issues there will be. The lesser the issues, the lower the possibility for fallout.

Chapter 7 – Finding the Right Place for Your Band to Practice

The ideal band practice space has an area to store your equipment between gigs and band practice. Finding a place to practice for your band is not an easy task. Being a new band you need to balance what you need with what is available and what the band can afford. If possible, you need to find a practice place with the following features:

- No stairs – so it will be easier for the band to carry the equipment

- Appropriate cooling and heating

- Have a good security lockup system to keep the equipment secured

- Located in an area convenient for all the band members

- Have proper electrical circuits

- Have proper insulation or sound barrier

Band Members' Homes

For bands that are just starting out, the most common place to practice is in the band member's garage or basement. At first, this starts out well, but as the time goes by the rest of the family members will be affected by the band practice. Several issues will arise like increased in utility bills, too noisy for the kids and neighbors, the equipment can take up a lot of space and others.

Storage Rental Units

Storage rental units may require the band to invest some money on it. But, if there are no other options available, this is a good place to consider. Before renting one make sure that you call around and compare prices as well as the contract. Make sure that you mention to the unit owner the reason why you renting the place, so they can determine if it will work for them to have a band practicing on their unit.

Rehearsal Studios

If the band has the capability or means to rent a studio why not rent one. It has everything you need - amplifiers, microphones, speakers, and mixers. It has a sound proof place to practice, a place where you can keep your equipment and sometimes you can rent their equipment as well. You have two options when renting a rehearsal studio – lockouts and hourly rentals.

Lockouts – it usually works like apartments. You need to sign a lease and pay a monthly fee. You can leave the band's equipment there; the room is yours only. Most of the lockouts are operating 24 hours a day, allowing you to use the facility anytime the band need to practice. If you know some band who are also looking for a place to practice you can share the room and the divide the expenses, this can lower your rental costs. The price of lockouts may differ greatly depending on location. The price may range from $200 to $500 per month.

Hourly Spaces – rehearsal studios may charge you for the number of hours you use the place. If the band is not rehearsing a lot or don't have enough money to rent, you are not forced to spend a lot of money every month. You need to check on the availability of the room. If all the rooms are occupied, then you have to wait. There are some rehearsal studios that allow the band to reserve the place earlier. You can also make some arrangements if you will be having regular practice. The rehearsal time is limited only, usually around two to fours only. The price may range from $10 to $30 per hour sometimes higher.

Chapter 8 – Musical Instruments You Need for Your Band

The instruments you need may vary depending on your band's chosen genre. As mentioned in Chapter 3, there are various types of bands and the instruments they play also vary.

Marching Bands

Marching bands use the following musical instruments – woodwind, percussion and brass instruments or other instruments that can be played and carried while walking. Some of the instruments marching bands use in their performances are as follows:

Brass instruments – cornet, trumpet, tuba, French horn

Woodwinds – clarinet, flute, oboe, saxophone Percussions – bass drum, cymbals, glockenspiel, Timpanis, xylophones

Symphonic Band

Symphonic band uses the same instruments that marching bands are using. The only difference is that symphonic band uses string instruments.

String instruments – banjo, cello, double bass, guitars, harp, lute, mandolin, ukulele, viola, violin and zithers.

Rock or Concert Band

Rock and roll music uses just about any instrument. Basically, a rock band will include drums, bass guitar and guitar. The range of instruments, though may include piano, woodwinds, accordion, mandolin, harmonica, cello, any type of percussion, banjo, fiddle or violin or any type of instrument.

Jazz Band

If you are putting up your own jazz band the instruments you need to have to create a unique and amazing blend of sound that only jazz music can produce are as follows – piano, saxophone, clarinet, trumpet.

Chapter 9 – How to Succeed as a Band

Now you have completed your band members, have the place to practice and have the budget, the next thing you should know is how to make success happen for your band. You have decided to get out of the garage and take the band's music career to a new level. But how you will be able to make these things possible. The path to success takes a lot of persistence, luck and dedication. Below are some of the things that will help you succeed, there is no easy way to make it as a band:

Ways to Improve Your Band

Consider ways to improve the band members' skills: jamming with others, fill in or play with other bands when possible, workshops, take musical retreats, invited musical guests, take courses or private tutoring, perform at events with other musicians, watch or read videos concerning musicians or music etc.

Know the Capabilities of Your Band Members

Are the band members satisfied with what they have reached? Know the things what the band members would like to contribute, perform, learn, do more of, or how they would like to participate even if they don't have the skills and then teach them, mentor them, work together so each member of the band advances each year. Give the band member a chance to succeed and fail, and succeed in new ways so that your band continues to evolve and fresh.

Practice More Often

Practice makes perfect. However, doing the same things again and again can make it tedious as well as very disappointing for everyone. Are you looking for ways to keep the material new and fresh? Maybe you can do something with the new songs so that you don't have to repeat the same show again and again, or learn something new regularly so that there is always a chance to see the music with new eyes.

Recording a Demo

Whether your band start with a song or a full album is one key to make your band known. Although, there are independent music cd venues out there, and several opportunities to access to a less expensive studio or home recording studio, if you have the resources and the chance to have a professionally produced product much better since it will sound better and with good quality.

Create a Press Kit

One of the important factors that will help your band succeed is to have a press kit also known as a promo kit. You will send the press kit to a concert and venue promoters, and to record label people in the future and to other organizations associated with the music industry. The kit typically includes demo, band photo and cover letter.

Create a Website

The internet is a no cost promotion machine and enables potential fans to listen to your music without wasting your money on buying blank CDs. Uploading your video online is free and easy, and millions of people can have free access to these sites. If people love your music it will go viral in an instant. Recording companies will notice your band's potential and might hire you in the future. You can use your website to promote your gigs and post new updates and provide information about your band. You can also promote your band in the discussion and forum boards of music sites that cater to the type of music you play.

Build a Fan Base

Aside from the music, the most essential part of being in a band is definitely the fans. Creating a fan base is a hard and long task. There is no guaranteed formula to win you fans. Trying every method is the best thing to do and think of some creative ideas to see what works for your band.

Get More Gigs

Once you have your press kit together, you are now prepared to get out there and start booking more gigs. The more gigs your band will play, the better it will be for your band. People will most likely to start taking notice. There are lots of venues that will not require you to have a full press kit, but it's essential to have it ready just in case.

Chapter 10 – Setting Goals and Assigning Tasks

You have chosen the band members, your band name and the general idea of what your band will sound like. Before you start your gig, you should determine the band's goals and the task each member will perform.

Share your ideas together with the other band members. Try to answer questions that may come up during the meeting and discuss any other concerns or ideas they might have.

Discuss among the members, who will write the songs. This can be done by one or two members. You should also discuss among your band members how often you will have your practice. The group should also decide on the show schedule, if you want to sign a record label or you want to go on tour.

Although roles and goals can change over time, the only way to keep organized is to establish them ahead of time. Go over your goals regularly and check how they may have changed.

Conclusion

Thank you again for purchasing this book!

I hope this book was able to help you start your own band. After reading this book, you will have a better idea that putting up a band can be an incredibly complex thing. Band members need to dedicate a lot of time to make things run smoothly. Fortunately, this book can help you a lot to make things easier. The primary point of being in a band is to enjoy, no matter how casual or serious your band may be.

Success takes time. The music industry is a tough business to break into, and it is filled with individuals who will take advantage of you, so be very careful in dealing with others.

Finally, if you enjoyed this book, then I'd like to ask you for a favor, would you be kind enough to leave a review for this book on Amazon? It'd be greatly appreciated!

Thank you and good luck!

Printed in Great Britain
by Amazon